The Ice Cream Carpet

for Mary Sansom

&

for Toby

Acknowledgements:

Some of these poems appeared in *Does W Trouble You?* (edited by Gerard Benson, Viking/Puffin), *Hello New* (edited by John Agard, Orchard Books), *The Guardian* newspaper and *The Rialto* magazine. Four of them appeared in Peter Sansom's Carcanet collections, *January* and *The Last Place On Earth*. Many thanks to the editors and publishers.

Also heartfelt thanks to the schools where many of these poems were started and/or tried out, to the brilliant teachers and their brilliant young poets.

The Ice Cream carpet

Poems by Peter Sansom
Illustrated by Ted Schofield

Smith/Doorstop Books

Published 2007 by
Smith/Doorstop Books
The Poetry Business
The Studio
Byram Arcade
Westgate
Huddersfield HD1 1ND

ISBN 9781902382784
A CIP catalogue record for this book is available from the British Library.

Designed and typeset at The Poetry Business
Printed and bound by CPI Antony Rowe, Eastbourne
Front cover design by Ted Schofield
Author photo by Mary Sansom

Distributed by Central Books Ltd., 99 Wallis Road, London E9 5LN

The Poetry Business gratefully acknowledges the help of Arts Council England and Kirklees Culture and Leisure Services.

CONTENTS

HEADTEACHER
WELCOME to our SCHOOL

I Opened the Door

I opened the door and walked through
I opened the door and stood in the doorway.
I opened the door and hit my head on the edge.
I opened the door no problem,
I've been opening doors all my life,
                    as long as I can remember.
I opened the door and went out,
It was raining.
I opened the door and went out,
It was sunny.
I opened the door and it wasn't raining or sunny,
It was a cupboard door.
I couldn't open the door, it was locked.
I couldn't open the door, it was bolted on the inside.
I couldn't open the door, it was a window.

The Giraffe from Hard-Up Zoo

A giraffe came into our class the other day
collecting for the zoo.
It said its name was Gervase
and it would tell us a story
if we would donate something
for the zoo.

We said ok and we all
got onto the carpet in the corner
even Mrs Birmingham
and waited for the story.
It was a really good story
about why giraffes have such long necks.

When it was finished
we all took a vote
and donated Mr Scott.

On My Bike

On my bike
on my bike
I go riding where I like.

Down the stairs
and through the hall,
while mum and dad
go up the wall.

At Uncle Mark's
and at my Gran's
I tear through the kitchen –
look, no hands!

On my bike
on my bike
I go riding where I like.

Round by the eggs
in the supermarket,
there's never any problem
trying to park it.

– Watch out, there's that cat!
Tring, tring, tring, tring!

On my bike
On my bike
I go riding where I like.

When I'm covered in sweat,
I'm not daft,
I go flat out
in a nice hot bath,

and at night
when it's locked in the shed,
I bike where I like
tucked up in bed.

On my bike
on my bike,
I go riding where I like.

Dear Vacuum Cleaner

I've got to go into town.
As a big favour would you
have a quick run round the house?

The living room is a pigsty.
Please be careful not to hoover up
any pigs or piglets.

Thank you.

PS

Don't bother with my bedroom,
a bomb hit it.

An Inventory of Inventions

The ice-cream carpet, that was one of mine.
And powdered water; winegum wine;
Jelly windows; see-through cats;
And yo-yo cornflakes, interstellar bobble-hats:
All mine. And mud television
And underwater sky,
Not to mention the Who What Why
Book of Bread. But the river of the
recent dead,
That was some other guy.

Dinosaurs

A nice bowl of cornflakes.
Go for the milk
and there is a dinosaur.
I close the fridge
and decide on toast.

Open the breadbin
and there's a dinosaur.
I slam the lid, I'm not hungry.

Some music.
Turn on the radio
and there is a dinosaur.
Not Radio One, not Radio Two or even Radio Four,
a dinosaur. Switch it off at the plug
and turn on the telly. The screen
is a diplodocus.

I'm late.
Hook my coat off the
pterodactyl in the hall
and open the front door

on a brontosaurus. Shut
the front door and go to the back

and there is another brontosaurus.
'Tyrannosaurus Rex, actually,' it says,
'we're quite easy to tell apart.'

Look at my watch.
Ten past the stegosaurus
and now way by that huge creature.
'Ah, but you're extinct,' I say.
'You're quite right,' he says,
and disappears.

Spike

Jack's got a dog
called Jasper
that can do tricks,
like fetch sticks.

Mum won't let me
have a dog. So I've got a dog
called Spike
who can ride a bike.

The New Boy

He picked a fight with himself and split his lip.
He poked himself in the back with a protractor.
He told tales on himself.
He threw his coat in the girls' toilets.
He made himself laugh in assembly
    and got called out to the front.
He nicked his maths book and wrote swearing all over it.
He nicked his ruler and wouldn't own up
    even though it had his initials on.
He flicked a rubber across the class and hit himself
                                        on the head.
He started bullying himself. No matter how early or late
    he was always there at the gates.
He copied off himself. He got bad marks.
He forgot somebody else's PE kit.
He drank his own milk while he wasn't looking.
He called himself names. 'Hey four eyes'
    though he didn't wear glasses.

The Woman in the Black Hat

A woman in a black hat
came into school, into our class.
I don't know why or where from.
Everybody was scared of her,
even Mr Watkins, you could tell.

She never said a word,
this tall woman in a hat,
and when she suddenly laughed
we sat very still.
I looked at Margaret
and she was trembling, like me,
and though everybody was like that

when she went out
we followed, the whole class,
single file,
into the library.
And there was the strangest thing:

all the books were reading themselves
out loud.
One after another at first,
and then all at once, very fast,
too many words to mean anything, until

one voice ended with the last sentence
of *The Tiger Who Came to Tea.*

At which
the big dictionary
flipped open and the leaves whirred
looking up a word and saying it and then another word
and every time it got there
the word disappeared
and soon

whole columns of words
disappeared
and the page was blank
and the more the pages turned
the more blank pages there were
till in the end the dictionary
was a notebook
and no words left in the world
for anyone to write.

We watched the woman go,
tipping her hat at the school gates
to the silenced headteacher,
the speechless caretaker,
the community policeman dumbfounded.

I'm Fat

I'm fat me, I get called names.
I'm tall for my age, I get called names.
Poor at our house, I get called names.
We're rich, my family, I get called names.
My family's from Pakistan, I get called names.
I wear glasses, I get called names.
Got red hair, I get called names.
Good in class, I get called names.
Got a wheelchair, me, I get called names.
Not from round here, I get called names.
Dad left home, I get called names.
A teacher me, I get called names.
A dinner lady, I get called names.
Deputy head, I get called names.
Head teacher, I get called names.
I'm hard, me.

A Cat in the Classroom

It just strolled in.
And no ordinary cat, either.
Somebody'd put a straw hat on it for a joke
or maybe somehow the cat itself
had got the doll's straw hat stuck on its head.

Some of us said the cat
was called Daisy, because of its hat
which had a plastic daisy in the brim.
Jonathan shouted
Daisy, Daisy, give me your answer do.
But the rest of us got down
on our knees and called Here cat,
here pussy cat, here little cat.

The caretaker called it
You Fleabag Moggy Get Out Of Here.
But that was later. Only ten minutes
till break and Mrs Tissiman
let it stay. It swam among the chairs, tiptoed
the tightrope of the bookcase top.
It didn't want to be stroked
or tickled under its chin.

We got on with our work
as if it wasn't there, then,
as if we could have a cat
in our classroom every day,
while it just sat on the high windowsill
behind Mrs T's desk,
washing its paws,
rather proud of its sun hat,
looking out at the rain.

The Day the School Bus Caught Fire

No-one was hurt though one or two instead of RE
or geography sat in sick bay nursing shock,
bags and blazers stitched with smoke,
while the road was blocked either end,
firemen round the blackened shell
like men with a beached whale.

When panic broke loose the kids shouted fire!
and the driver reasonably ignored them,
till flames and fumes filled his mirror and stopped the bus,
and a rumour spread the fuel tank would go;
then the doors and emergency door opened
and they piled out white-faced and elated

to be counted at a safe distance –
safe: from the four walls where a parent's world ends. Safe:
the driver free in time to make a joke at the depot
and the bell telling the kids like any other day
where to be with done or not-done homework,
the felt-tipped hearts of who loves whom

and games last thing to dread or look forward to,
in friendship and rivalry closer today

than they will ever be again –
a day that will just pop into their heads
miles from here, decades, today,
the day the school bus caught fire.

You Will Soon Get Warm As You Run Up and Down

The teacher's in that cute
sporty bright pink tracksuit

and under it
you know she's got on
her thermal shorts
and thermal longjohns,
her thermal shirt
and thermal vest
like for an assault
on Everest.

Have you guessed?
Well, this'll help you crack it,
she's putting on her sheepskin jacket,

her hands are mittens
round a mug of tea
and she stamps her feet
continually

while the boys and girls
run out for sports
in thin white shirts
and thin white shorts

their thin white arms
and thin white legs
like bits of string
with knots in
shivering
and as they do
turning blue.

we're off in a rocket

we're off in a rocket
in a rocket to the sky
put your space suit on
put your space suit on

we're off in a rocket
in a shuttle to the moon
put your space suit on
put your helmet on

we're off in a rocket
in a shuttle to the moon
put your helmet on
put your space gloves on

we're off in a rocket
in a shuttle to the moon
with our space suit on
and our space gloves on
and our helmet on
and the visor down

put your seat belt on
put your seat belt on
and prepare yourself
for blast off

we're off in a rocket
through the black black sky
we're off in a rocket
in a shuttle to the moon

5
4
3
2
1
BLAST OFF!

I Listened

I listened to my mum,
I listened to my dad,
I listened to my sister
although my sister's mad.

I listened to my uncle,
I listened to my aunt,
though the only thing that they can say
is Mustn't, Don't and Can't.

I listened like a good boy
to every thing they said.
I listened to my grandad,
although my grandad's dead.

I listened to my brother
and my brother's stupid friend,
though everybody knows
that they're both round the bend.

I listened to my teacher
and the headteacher's advice.
But today I'll say something myself,
and it won't be very nice.

Letter to Grandad's Stairs

I've noticed you can't
drag yourself
all the way up
any more. You stop
three steps
from the top.

When it was one
that was all right.

He could manage.
And when it was two
that was fine too.
But three. Three's hard.

Not coming down, He can
jump. Like he says,
he's not an invalid.
But, like he says,
three's getting beyond him,
he's not as young as he was.

And what happens next week
or the week after
when you're short of
four steps or five?
Coming down will be dangerous.
What happens one day

you stop half way?

Something will have to be done
like Grandad says
if something can be done.

The Highwayman

The highwayman lives for the moment he shouts
STAND AND DELIVER!
He waits among the trees,
a shadow in the shadows,
his black cloak, his black mask.

It's time. The moon comes clear of cloud
and he steps out on to the roadside.
The coach is nearer each moment.
Until the highwayman shouts
STAND AND DELIVER!
caught for a moment in the headlights.

The coachdriver blares his horn,
GET OUT OF THE WAY YOU LUNATIC!
and indicates to join the motorway.
The highwayman shakes his fist
at the world changed,
at how robbery has moved on,

and melts again into the dripping trees,
the aimless paths of the wood,
a shadow among shadows,
his money, his life.

MA

Mrs Sansom's Proud Giraffe

It sings and dances
and gives shy glances,
Mrs Sansom's proud giraffe.
Its neck so long and slender,
its voice so sweet and tender,
who'd have thought it is a football fan,
Mrs Sansom's proud giraffe.

It sings of love and pain and stuff
and wears his blue and yellow scarf
on its way to games away and home,
Mrs Sansom's proud giraffe.
It sings Away the lads, and dances,
Mrs Sansom's proud giraffe.

On the terraces of Mansfield Town
it dances up and up and up and down,
Mrs Sansom's proud giraffe,
Mrs Sansom's very fine and proud giraffe.

Icarus

Daedalus and his son, that parable,
forget it.
It's not about flying too high
but about flying at all.

The son died.
The father lived with his remorse,
Tell me which you think is worse.

Do you really think that ingenious father
imagined for a moment that wax would do?
That man used glue.

Do you think, as the son got close to the sun,
the wax melted,
the wings fell apart
and Icarus fell through all those storeys of blue
into the sea?

Not warmth, but ice on the wings
brought him down
brought him spiralling down

where he belonged.

Looking

I looked in the kitchen
but it wasn't the right place,
there were only kitchen things.
The rest was kitchen space.

I looked in my bedroom
and my brother's room next door –
there were cheesy socks under the bed
by the grinning head of a dinosaur.

I looked in the new-tiled bathroom,
there were seven shades of blue
and just towels and soap and toothbrushes
and an indigo low-flush loo.

Then I tried in the garage,
but all there was in there
was my dad's trusty Rover
that gave up the ghost last year.

Which was when I remembered the attic.
I climbed to its sloping gloom,
and there at the dormer window

was the outside's living room.

Looking through miles of rain
across at Castle Hill,
I found I could sit and stare
beyond myself. And be still.

Umbrella Weather

I love this
umbrella weather,
really pouring, but straight down
and not so windy
to turn it inside out
or lift us Mary Poppins off our feet.

I love this
umbrella weather,
when I'm hugged into Dad,
though I'm up to his shoulder
(old enough to go on my own)
like one person under

our brilliant yellow travelling tent
that drums like the Lake District,
when we cross the river
of Minna Road with the green man,
wipers going like a monsoon on the bus
that's stopped for us

in our own brilliant yellow world
of stepping round puddles
and other umbrellas
the long short walk to school,
and we agree, Dad and me,
that we love

this umbrella weather.

The Settee in Autumn

Leaves change colour and fall on the russet settee.
Sticky buds are stuck down the back of the settee
with coins and old biros.

The last, unpicked blackberries are left to rot
on the settee. A little acorn is starting the long, almost
motionless journey

to becoming a mighty settee. Three tins of Weightwatcher
Tomato Soup
are brought to the harvest festival on the settee.

All across the country, anti-freeze is poured into settees
but still in the dark mornings many settees refuse to start:

Jump leads are attached and running neighbours laughing
let go of bumpstarted settees.

Dank mists. Fir cones and icing-sugar spiders-webs
on the settee.

Two die in apple-bobbing drama on settee.
A flickering candle in the pumpkin head on the settee.

There is Guy Fawkes on the settee.
There are settees sitting on settees
on the blazing bonfire of the settees.

Imagine Being a Nose

Imagine being a nose,
smelling all the time and no one saying BATH!!

Imagine those fish and chips
and never able to eat them.

Catching a cold: running everywhere,
red and exhausted. Sneezing when you least ex

tishoo.
Imagine being a nose,

sniffing at everything
you get pointed at:

those socks. Those underpants.
Under that arm.

Never any choice.
Always getting picked.

Nogard Dnuoblleps
Hslew ma I
Emalf dna ekoms ni klat I tub
Dlog dna revlis tnilg selacs ym
Sselesu era sgniw ym
Rorrim siht morf em kcolnu uoy litnu
Ekal eht ni em denword draziw eht
em dnif
em eerf
em ni eveileb

Monster

And do you know what I'm frightened of?

The boy trembled but didn't run.
The monster roared with laughter. One hairy arm
snaked out to pat the boy's head.
Guess, it said, *Guess what I'm scared of.*

The boy's mouth was dry.
He couldn't speak. Lightning
lit up the stairwell, the whole estate.
'Thunderstorms,' the boy said.
The monster roared with laughter.
No, I cause thunderstorms.
A clap of thunder bounded to them up the stairs.

'Ghosts', the boy said, desperate.
The monster grinned.
No, I'm not scared of ghosts
because I am a ghost. See.
And its skin went transparent
and it pulled out
its beating heart.
I'm quite dead, it said. *Or quite undead.*

The boy felt sick.

If he could just get away,
he'd always go straight home.
Why had he come out to the old flats?

The monster pushed its melting face
in the boy's face. *What am I afraid of?*
Tell me that, and I'll let you go.
But the boy didn't know.
And so the boy took a breath, and said

'You're scared of your mum and dad fighting.'
The monster roared with laughter.
No, I'm not scared of that because
I am *your mum and dad fighting. Watch –*

'Bats, then,' the boy said quickly,
'when it starts to get dark, like down the rec,
and Count Dracula.' And then before
the monster could reply, the boy
realised the monster's questions were really a ploy.

'What you're most afraid of,' the boy said,
'is a boy who looks you in the eye
and says *Yes, I am scared,*
but I'm not scared of you.'
And then the boy turned and walked
down the stairs and out into the street,
careful not to look back.

Beachcombing My Room

Monday I found a donkey jacket
on the back of my chair, and a donkey
standing there. I've always
wanted a donkey.

Tuesday there was an atlas
the size of my desk, brilliant and alive
with colour. I spent the day
in blue-white Antarctica.

Wednesday: a perfect pyramid
of horse droppings or possibly
donkey. I took a spade
and hoofed them out the window.

Thursday there was my dad
asleep on the rug.
I haven't seen my dad for years.
I took a photo and tiptoed out.

Friday – nothing.
I was fed up, ate hobnobs
till I felt sick, watched telly,
watched the rain.

Saturday there was a wardrobe
next to my wardrobe. I stepped in
among the coats. And strode through amazed
into Rotherham.

Sunday like everyone
I went to the shopping *mall*
and bought everything I could afford
and quite a bit I couldn't. Back home,

it was Monday again.
I could hardly get into my room
and when I did I found this coat.
Is it yours, Donkey?

A useful pocket guide to all the major roads in Britain
A

Mr & Mrs Highwayman

'Your money or your life!' he yelled.
'I thought you'd never ask,' she said, blushing.
And within the week they were married.
And over time she took to black –
a midnight cloak, a moonless tunic
and boots that shone with darkness.
In turn he learned to live without his mask
and gave up, more or less, accosting
strangers at pistolpoint.

'How will we live, Mrs H?'
'Happily,' said she, 'ever after.
We will be characters in books
and now and then a film and the tellybox.
The money will roll in.'
Which is how it should be and would be and is.